SPIDER-MAN 2

**Based on the screenplay by
Alvin Sargent**

**Screen Story by
Alfred Gough & Miles Millar and
Michael Chabon**

**Based on the Marvel Comic Book
by Stan Lee and Steve Ditko**

LEVEL 2

Adapted by: Jane Rollason

Commissioning Editor: Helen Parker

Editor: Clare Gray

Cover layout: Emily Spencer

Designer: Victoria Wren

Picture research: Emma Bree

Photo credits:
Cover image and inside photos provided courtesy Columbia Pictures Industries, Inc.
Page 48: J. Romita/Marvel/Corbis.
Page 50: S. Sollfors, Blickwinkel/Alamy.
Page 53: P. Parks/AFP/Getty Images.

Published by Scholastic Ltd 2007

Printed in Singapore. Reprinted in 2008.
This edition printed in 2009.

CONTENTS

SPIDER

Peter Parker is just an ordinary guy. He has problems with money and girls. He's in love with MJ, but can he ever be with her?
Peter Parker is also Spider-Man. He swings through the streets of New York and saves people from danger. Sometimes New Yorkers call him 'Spidey'.

Dr Otto Octavius is a brilliant scientist with big ideas. His life's work is fusion energy – cheap, safe energy for everyone.

Mary Jane Watson (MJ) works in the theatre and her face is famous in New York. MJ had a difficult home life. Now she has left home and she's a strong young woman. She has faced all her problems, except one – her feelings for Peter Parker.

...AN 2™

Harry Osborn is Peter's best friend. He thinks Spider-Man killed his father. Harry's father died in a fight with Spider-Man. His father was trying to kill Spider-Man at the time. But Harry doesn't know this and now he wants to kill Spider-Man.

Aunt May is like a mother to Peter. She lives alone. Her husband, Uncle Ben, died two years ago. A criminal killed him when he tried to take Uncle Ben's car. She has money problems and she's still sad about Uncle Ben. But she's a very strong person.

Doctor Octopus (Doc Ock) is a dangerous, crazy scientist with four metal arms. He wants to use fusion energy – but not for the good of the world!

PLACES

Manhattan is the centre of New York City. All the biggest shops, tallest buildings and most famous places are here.

The Planetarium is a beautiful, modern building next to Central Park.

Thousands of Chinese people live and work in New York's **Chinatown**.

The Westside Tower is a very tall building with a big clock.

The Hudson River runs past Manhattan to the sea.

Forest Hills is in Queens, outside Manhattan. Aunt May lives here.

SPIDER-MAN 2™

Chapter 1
Late again

She looks at me every day. Mary Jane Watson. Her picture is all over New York. I love her. But she doesn't know – she can never know. She can't be part of my life. Who am I? I'm Spider-Man and I have an important job to do. I'm also Peter Parker, and I too have a job to do …

Peter stopped his bike outside Joe's Pizza bar. His boss, Mr Aziz, was standing outside.

'Parker!' he shouted. 'You're late! Always late!'

Mr Aziz turned around. On the back of his t-shirt it said, '*29 minutes or it's free!*' Peter followed Mr Aziz inside the busy pizza bar.

'This order came in twenty-one minutes ago,' Mr Aziz explained, pointing at the big Joe's Pizzas clock. He passed eight pizza boxes to Peter. 'You've got seven and a half minutes … or you'll lose your job! GO!'

Peter rode his bike through the cars, taxis and buses on Manhattan's busy streets. He saw a clock on a street corner. Three minutes to two! He had just three minutes left! There was only one thing to do. He left his bike and ran into a small street. He quickly changed into his Spider-Man clothes. Then he shot a line of webbing and swung into the street. A man saw him and shouted, 'Hey! Spidey's taken that guy's pizzas!'

Some New Yorkers didn't like Spider-Man much. There were bad stories about him in the *Daily Bugle*, the city newspaper, nearly every day. And people believed them.

Spider-Man swung from building to building. Not much time left! But then two young children ran out into a busy street.

Peter put the pizza boxes on a building. He swung down and took the children in his arms. He pulled them to the other side of the street – just in time. The little boy and girl looked at him with big eyes.

'No playing in the street,' Spider-Man said to them.

'Yes, Mr Spider-Man,' they answered.

He collected the pizzas and went into an office building. It was three minutes past two. 'You're late,' said the woman behind the desk. 'I'm not paying for those.'

Peter lost his job at Joe's Pizza bar, but he still had work at the *Daily Bugle*. He took pictures of Spider-Man for the newspaper. He went to see the top man at the paper, Jonah Jameson. Peter wanted to sell photos of other things – birds in the park, faces of interesting old men. But Jonah Jameson wasn't interested.

'I only pay you because you take pictures of Spider-Man!' he shouted.

'Spider-Man won't let me take any more pictures,' said Peter. 'The city hates him because of you.'

'Well, I don't want your other pictures.'

'OK,' said Peter, and he pulled out a fantastic photo of Spider-Man.

'I'll give you a hundred and fifty,' said Jameson.

'Three hundred,' said Peter.

'OK, OK,' said Jameson. 'Go and see Betty.'

Peter went to get the money from Betty Brandt. Betty worked for Mr Jameson.

'You borrowed some money two weeks ago,' she said kindly, 'I can't give you any more … Sorry.'

'Oh no!' thought Peter, 'I'm late again.' He ran to the university. He ran faster than any ordinary person. People were looking at him but he didn't care. He turned a corner and ran into someone. Books and papers flew everywhere. Peter took the books and papers in his hands and stood up – right in front of his teacher!

'Oh, Dr Connors! Sorry!' he said.

'Where were you going, Parker?'

'To your class.'

'My class is over,' said Dr Connors. 'Look at you, Peter. You're always late for class. You're always so tired. Your homework on fusion is late.'

'I know … ,' said Peter, 'I'm planning to write my fusion homework on Dr Otto Octavius.'

'Octavius is a friend of mine. Make sure it's good.'

It was dark when Peter arrived at Aunt May's house in Forest Hills. He walked into the living room. He was thinking about other things and he didn't see Aunt May, MJ and Harry standing there …

Chapter 2
Happy birthday!

'Surprise!' they shouted.

'What's happening?' asked Peter.

'It's your birthday!' said Aunt May.

'Long time no see,' said MJ.

'MJ!' said Peter. 'How's the play?'

'She's brilliant in it,' said Harry.

'Harry sent me flowers,' said MJ, quietly. She smiled at Peter, then she looked away. 'I'll go and get the food.'

Peter turned to Harry. 'So … how are things going at OsCorp*?' he asked.

'Great,' said Harry. 'I'm Head of Special Ideas. We're doing some brilliant new work on fusion. Dr Otto

* The Osborn Corporation: a big scientific business. Harry's father Norman Osborn started OsCorp.

Octavius is working for us. Maybe you'd like to meet him?'

'Great! I'm writing about his work for Dr Connors,' Peter smiled.

Then Harry's face changed. 'MJ's waiting for you, Peter,' he said. 'The way she looks at you …'

'I don't have time for girls right now,' said Peter. 'I'm very busy.'

'Taking pictures of your friend, Spider-Man?' asked Harry.

'Can we talk about something else?' said Peter. 'I want us to be friends, Harry.'

'If you know who he is, Peter, please tell me.'

Peter didn't answer. He couldn't answer. Harry's father died in a fight with Spider-Man and Harry hated him. But Peter *was* Spider-Man. What could he do?

Aunt May was asleep in a chair. There were some letters on the table. One was from the bank. It wasn't good news.

Peter woke her.

'What … Ben? Oh, Peter,' she said. 'Has everybody gone? Did they have a good time?'

'I'm sure they did,' Peter smiled. Then his face changed. 'Aunt May, I saw the letter from the bank.'

'You did? Oh, well … I'm a little behind. I don't want to talk about it any more. I'm tired.'

She took $20 from her bag. 'Happy birthday, Peter,' she said.

'Aunt May, I can't take this from you.'

'Yes, you can,' she said angrily. 'You can take this money from me. It's not much!' Then she started crying. 'I'm sorry. Life is so empty without your Uncle Ben. It's nearly two years since he died. Sometimes I think about his killer … and I want to do something terrible.'

Uncle Ben's killer was dead. The police didn't know that. Aunt May didn't know that. But Peter knew. He was there and he saw everything. He looked at poor Aunt May and he felt so bad. He wanted to tell her but he couldn't.

'Here!' she said. 'Take some birthday cake home.'

Before he went home, Peter went into Aunt May's garden.

'Hey,' said MJ. She was in her parents' garden next door.

'I saw your picture on Bleecker Street*,' said Peter.

'Oh, isn't it funny?' she said. MJ didn't like seeing her picture all around New York.

'No! It's nice,' he said. 'I can see you every day now.'

He loved MJ. But he couldn't tell her. It wasn't fair. Anyone close to Spider-Man was always in danger.

'Do you want to say something?' asked MJ.

'I … er … are you still living in Manhattan?'

'Oh, Peter …' she said sadly. 'I don't understand you.'

MJ walked back to the house. Then she turned. 'I'm seeing someone now.'

'You mean a boyfriend?'

Suddenly Peter wanted to show MJ his feelings.

'I'm going to come to your play tomorrow night.'

She was surprised. 'You're coming?'

'I'll be there,' he said.

Peter went home to his little room. It was at the top of an

* A street in the centre of New York.

old house in Manhattan. Peter walked slowly up the stairs.

'Money!' shouted Mr Ditkovitch. It was his house and he lived on the floor below Peter.

'Hi,' said Peter.

'What's "Hi"? Can I spend it?'

'Mr Ditkovitch. I'll get some more money this week …'

'You're a month late with the money for the room. Again!'

'But I only have this $20 for the week,' Peter explained.

Mr Ditkovitch took Peter's $20 – his birthday money – and shut the door.

Peter went into his cold little room and sat on the bed.

'Could things be any worse?' he thought.

Chapter 3
Fusion

Dr Otto Octavius was working in a special room at home. It was in a lovely old building with big windows. Harry walked in, followed by Peter. Otto stopped his work and walked towards the two young men. He was a big man with a kind face. He smiled warmly at Harry, then turned towards Peter.

'This is my good friend, Peter Parker,' Harry explained. 'I called you about him. I only got through my school science exams because of Peter.'

Peter smiled at Otto. 'I'm studying your work at university,' Peter said.

'I have to go,' Harry said, moving towards the door. 'I've got an important meeting. I'll leave you two clever scientists together … and good luck tomorrow, Otto!'

'Parker?' said Otto. 'I remember now. You're Connors' student … He tells me you're brilliant … but lazy.'

'I'm trying to do better,' said Peter.

Otto was serious now. 'Being brilliant isn't enough,' he explained. 'You have to work hard – and you must use science for the good of the world.'

Otto showed Peter his work on fusion – a new kind of cheap energy. Enough energy for everyone in the world! Peter asked lots of intelligent questions. Later, after coffee, the two men were still talking about fusion. Otto's wife, Rosie, was there, too.

'Are you sure you can control the fusion reaction?' asked Peter, at last.

'Peter! This is my life's work. The city isn't in danger.'

'Otto's done his homework,' said Rosie. And they all laughed.

Chapter 4
An empty seat

MJ was finishing her make-up in the dressing room at the theatre. She looked at herself in the mirror.

'Will he come?' she thought.

A man's face appeared at the dressing room door. 'Five minutes! Five minutes!' he called. Then he was gone.

Peter was on his bike and he was nearly at the theatre. Suddenly, a big car drove up behind him very fast. 'Jump up!' his spider sense told him. Peter jumped high above the car. His bike fell under the car and broke into pieces. A moment later, he was standing safely on his feet again.

'How did you do that?' asked a boy at the side of the road.

'I do a lot of exercise,' Peter said, 'and I eat my green vegetables.'

'My mother always says that,' said the boy. 'I just never believed her.'

The big car was driving very fast up the road now. A gunman was shooting out of the back of the car at the police.

'Why can't I have just one night off?' thought Peter.

Suddenly two police cars crashed into each other. One of the cars flew up high above some people. They cried out as the car fell towards them. But then it stopped still. It didn't hit the people! Everyone looked at the car above them. Something was holding the car there.

'It's a web!' said a woman.

Suddenly, something blue and red swung over their heads.

'Go, Spidey, go!' the woman shouted.

The men in the big car saw him. They both started shooting at Spider-Man. Peter was really angry. He wanted to be at the theatre. He jumped onto the back of the car. He shot webbing at the two men, then pulled them out of the car.

Next, he pulled the webbing over a street light and the men were hanging high above the road. Peter jumped into the driver's seat and drove the car to the theatre.

MJ wasn't having a good night. She wasn't thinking about the play, she was thinking about one of the best seats in the theatre. Peter's seat. It was empty.

Peter walked into the theatre and pulled his ticket from his pocket. He showed it to the man at the door.

'Sorry,' said the man. He pointed to a sign. 'You can't go in when the doors are closed,' he explained.

Peter crossed the road and waited opposite the theatre.

MJ came out after the play. She looked up and down the street. No Peter.

'Could you sign here, please?' said a good-looking young man.

'What are you doing here?' smiled MJ.

It was John – MJ's new boyfriend. He put his arms around her and they kissed.

A police car drove by fast. Then another and another.

'Are you hungry?' John asked.

'Yes,' smiled MJ. 'Very!'

On the other side of the road, Peter watched sadly as MJ and John hurried away. Then he remembered the police cars.

'Why do I always have to rescue people from fires and criminals?' he thought. 'I only wanted one evening at the theatre.'

He changed his clothes in a small street. He ran up the side of a building and jumped onto the roof. For the first time ever, he didn't want to do it. But he was Spider-Man. He had to do it! Soon he was swinging from building to building towards the police cars. He brought his arm around to shoot a line of webbing … but nothing happened. Spider-Man was high above the street with no webbing. 'Aaaagh!' he cried as he crashed down onto a building below.

He stood up slowly and looked down. Then he looked at his hands and tried to shoot some webbing. Nothing. 'What's happening to me?' he thought.

Five minutes later, he was in a lift. A man with a dog got in.

'Cool Spidey clothes,' the man said.

'Thanks,' said Peter.

All through Dr Connors' class Peter thought about MJ. After the class, he phoned her from the university. There was no answer so he left a message.

'Hi, MJ, this is Peter. I was on my way to your show… and, well, I was on my bike … er … Are you there? I've been thinking about it all day and …'

CLICK! The phone cut off. Peter didn't have any more money, but he continued, 'I want to tell you the truth,' he said. 'Here it is. I am Spider-Man. So … I can't be with you. A lot of people want to kill me … I can't put you in danger. I think about you every day. I really want to tell you … but I can't.'

MJ wasn't going to hear the last bit. Peter knew this, but he wanted to say it anyway.

Chapter 5
The metal arms

About forty visitors waited excitedly in Otto's big room. Harry and Peter were there.

'Welcome, everyone,' said Otto. 'You are the first people ever to see fusion energy. It's safe – and we can make it again and again. It's cheap, too. Cheap electricity for everyone!' Otto moved across the room towards four big metal arms.

'Ooooooh,' everyone said as Otto fitted the arms onto his back. 'It's not possible to control the fusion reaction with my hands. So I use these metal ones. I control them with my brain,' he explained.

'Dr Octavius,' asked one of the visitors, 'is there a danger the arms can control *you*?'

'Good question,' said Otto. 'My brain is safe because of this microchip at the back of my head.' He turned and showed them. 'I control the arms,' he said. 'They don't control me.'

Otto walked to the back of the room. Blue lights went on and there was Otto's fusion reactor. The metal arms moved. They lifted up a very small piece of tritium*. 'There are less than twelve kilos of tritium in the world,' he explained. 'I want to thank Harry Osborn and OsCorp for giving me this tritium.'

'Happy to pay the bills, Otto,' called Harry.

Otto turned to smile at his wife, Rosie. This was his big moment! He started the reaction. The tritium started to go round very fast. Suddenly it changed into a small ball of fire. It started to grow. The light was very strong. The visitors couldn't believe it. The energy of the sun was in the room in front of them.

Otto used the metal arms to control the reaction. Lines of fire shot from the fireball. The arms stopped each one and pushed it back to the centre. The arms moved faster and faster, and the light became stronger and stronger.

But then something happened. The reactor started to pull some of the metal things in the room into its centre. Lines of fire shot everywhere. Otto was losing control. People shouted and tried to escape. Harry's face was white. He turned towards Peter. But Peter wasn't there.

'Turn it off!' shouted Harry. 'Turn it off!'

'Wait!' shouted Otto. 'I can control it.'

A big metal cupboard was flying towards Harry. But suddenly Spider-Man appeared. He caught Harry and pulled him away from danger. For a moment, Spider-Man and Harry were face to face. But Harry still hated Spider-Man.

* Tritium can be dangerous. Scientists use it for fusion reactions.

'This doesn't change anything,' Harry said.

But Spider-Man didn't have time to talk. He ran around the walls to the reactor. He tried to pull the cables out of the wall.

'What are you doing?' shouted Otto.

'I'm trying to stop the reaction,' answered Spider-Man.

One of Otto's metal arms hit Spider-Man. But at that moment the big windows in the room broke into a thousand pieces. Metal and glass flew fast towards Otto and Rosie. The metal arms moved in front of Otto's body. He was safe. But Rosie fell to the floor.

'Rosie!' shouted Otto.

Then a line of fire from the reactor hit Otto in the back. He fell to the floor. Smoke came out of the microchip.

Spider-Man pulled and pulled. Finally the cables came out of the wall. The reactor stopped. The lights went out. Everything went quiet.

Otto's body showed signs of life. They took him to hospital. But it was too late for Rosie.

Harry stood in the street outside. His car was waiting but he didn't get in.

'I've lost everything,' he said. 'I've nothing – except Spider-Man.'

'But he saved your life,' said one of the OsCorp men.

'He made me look stupid today. He'll pay for this.'

Harry got in his car and left.

Chapter 6
Doc Ock

Otto was on a big table in the hospital theatre. The doctors were ready.

'OK,' said Dr Isaacs. 'We need to take off these metal arms.'

He moved towards the first metal arm with a knife. But then he stopped – the arm was 'looking' at him. Then suddenly the arm hit Dr Isaacs very hard. He flew across the room and crashed through a window. Then the arms turned to the other doctors and killed them, too.

Otto woke up and looked around. He was in a hospital theatre. And then he saw bodies, blood and glass everywhere.

'No!' he cried. All this was his fault. The arms were killers – and he couldn't stop them!

Otto tried to stand. The arms helped him. Two of the arms became legs. They walked out of the hospital and into the road. A taxi was going to crash into them! But the arms hit the taxi and it turned over.

They went down to the Hudson River. There they found an empty old building above the water. The arms had some dark plans. This was a great place to make them real!

'Everyone's talking about it!' cried Jonah Jameson, in his office at the *Daily Bugle*. 'A crazy scientist with four metal arms. What do we call him?' he shouted.

'Dr Octopus*?' said one of his men.

'Dr Octopus! Doc Ock! I love it.'

Betty Brandt brought Peter into the office.

'Where have you been?' Jameson shouted. 'There's a crazy scientist in town and we have no pictures! You've lost your job!'

'Boss … the Planetarium party …' said Betty.

'Oh … erm … OK, Parker, I need you. There's a big party for an American hero … my son!'

'Could you pay me now?' asked Peter.

* *An octopus lives in the sea and has eight legs.*

Jameson laughed loudly. Then he looked at Peter again and laughed some more.

'Planetarium! Tomorrow night. Eight o'clock. Goodbye!'

Down on the river, Otto was sitting all alone. 'My Rosie's dead,' he said. 'My dream is dead …' He looked down sadly at the water.

'Something is talking in my brain,' he thought. He put his hand to the back of his head. The microchip was gone! 'Peter was right,' Otto said. 'I couldn't control the reaction.'

But then the voice in his brain got louder. 'It was working,' it said. 'We can build the reactor again!'

'Yes,' said Otto. 'We'll build again! We need money! We will take money! It's a crime not to finish our work.' The arms were taking control of his brain now.

'The energy of the sun in my hands!' cried Otto. 'Nothing will stand in our way! Nothing!'

'No,' said the man at the bank. 'We can't lend you any money.'

'I see,' said Aunt May. She smiled, but she sounded tired and old.

Peter took her hand. 'Don't worry. We'll find a way,' he said.

But then … 'Oh no!' he thought. His spider sense woke up.

Doc Ock arrived at the bank! He was wearing a big coat and dark glasses. He wanted money, too. But he wasn't going to ask for it. The long arms came out of his coat. They pulled off a big metal door at the back of the bank.

They threw the door across the bank towards Peter and Aunt May.

Peter ran to change his clothes.

'Don't leave me!' called Aunt May.

Spider-Man ran around the walls behind Doc Ock. The arms threw bags of money at him. Peter tried to shoot some webbing, but nothing happened. A bag of money hit Peter and he fell to the floor.

The metal arms lifted him up. Two metal hands pushed down on his head.

Now Peter was angry! He shot webbing to the right and left. He pulled two heavy desks fast towards Ock. Doc Ock and a desk crashed through the bank window. People on the street outside cried out. At that moment two police cars arrived. The police jumped out and pointed their guns at Ock.

A metal arm moved towards a crowd of people and took a woman in its hand. It was Aunt May! She had an umbrella in her hand and she hit Ock with it.

'Don't follow me!' Ock shouted. And he ran up the side of a high building. The police couldn't shoot at Ock because he had Aunt May in his arms.

Spider-Man was waiting near the top of the building. 'Give her to me,' he said. At first Ock lifted Aunt May up to Spider-Man, but then he opened his metal hand. Now Aunt May was falling fast! In a moment, Spider-Man shot webbing at Aunt May and stopped her fall. Ock hit Spider-Man and Aunt May swung back up. She hung onto the building with her umbrella!

Ock and Spider-Man fought up and down the building. Ock threw Spider-Man through a window of a building across the street. Peter shot webbing at both sides of the window. He pulled back on the webbing and fired himself across to Ock and Aunt May.

Ock held Aunt May behind his back. A long knife came out of one of the arms. Suddenly Aunt May swung her umbrella into Ock's face. His dark glasses broke and he cried out. He dropped Aunt May – again! But Spider-Man shot two lines of webbing down to Aunt May and quickly caught her. He swung down to the street and put her down very carefully. Aunt May wasn't in danger now, so the police started to shoot at Ock. But Ock went higher up the building and escaped over the roof.

Chapter 7
Spider-Man no more

Harry sat at the bar in the Planetarium.

'You're drinking too much, Harry,' said Peter.

'It's a party,' said Harry, 'And don't forget I've just lost all my money on a crazy scientist. And then there's Spider-Man.'

'Let's not talk about him tonight, Harry.'

'Every night, Peter,' said Harry. 'Until I find him I can only think about Spider-Man.'

'PARKER!' shouted Jonah Jameson across the room. 'Parker, I'm not paying you to sit at the bar all evening. Take photos. Take more photos. Take pictures of me and my wife with the city's most important people.'

Just then a woman spoke into a microphone.

'Good evening, everyone,' she said. 'Tonight the Science Library of New York welcomes a special American hero – the first man to play football on the Moon. The great, the fine, the good-looking Captain John Jameson!'

The band played and John Jameson came down some stairs. Peter was ready with his camera. But he couldn't take the picture. MJ was standing next to John Jameson, with her arm in his.

She smiled as she looked at all the faces. But then she saw Peter.

Later Peter found MJ outside the party.

'Hi,' he said.

'Oh, you,' she said.

'Listen, I'm sorry,' he said. 'There was trouble on the way to the theatre–' She stopped him.

'I don't know you,' she said angrily. 'And I can't think about you any more. It hurts too much.'

'Can I get you a drink?'

'I'm with John. He'll get my drink … John has seen my show five times. Harry has seen it. Aunt May has seen it. My ill mother has seen it. Even my father has seen it. But my best friend … oh no, he can't get to a theatre for eight o'clock. After all these years, he's just an empty seat to me.'

A little later John Jameson took the microphone. 'I just want you all to know,' he said. 'The beautiful Miss Mary Jane Watson has just agreed to be my wife.'

MJ went up to John and kissed him.

'Shoot the picture, Parker!' said Jonah Jameson. 'Shoot the picture!'

Peter lifted the camera and took the picture. But he could only think about MJ. Was she lost to him now?

He ran outside. He changed into his Spider-Man clothes

and started to swing through the city. He felt better. But not for long – suddenly there was no more webbing! He crashed down to the street. He tried again to shoot some webbing, but nothing happened. 'Why's this happening to me?' he asked. He tried to go up a wall, but he crashed down again. He sat there for a moment. He saw an old *Daily Bugle* next to him. His Spider-Man photo was on the front page. The story was about Spider-Man and Doc Ock at the bank – they were taking the money *together*!

Late that night there was a storm in the city. Peter couldn't sleep. He was thinking about Uncle Ben. He thought about Uncle Ben's words – the words he said on the day he died: *'With great power comes great responsibility.'**

'I can't live your dreams any more, Uncle Ben,' said Peter. 'I can't be Spider-Man. I want a life of my own.'

Peter got dressed. He took his Spider-Man clothes with him and went out. He came to a small street and threw his Spider-Man clothes away.

'Spider-Man no more,' he thought. And he went home.

---

* Peter must think carefully before he does something. And he must always do the right thing.

Chapter 8
An ordinary life

Peter sat in the theatre and watched MJ. He was enjoying the play so much! At one moment MJ saw Peter. They smiled at each other and for a few seconds she forgot her lines.

After the play, they walked through Chinatown together.

'You were so wonderful,' he said.

'You look … different,' she said.

'Well, I cleaned my shoes. I washed my clothes. I did my homework. I do my homework now. Do you want to get some Chinese food?'

'Peter … I'm getting married.'

'You once said to me, "I love you." Back then, I couldn't be with you. There were things I had to do. But I don't have to do them now.'

'You're too late,' she said.

'Will you think about it?'

'Think about what?'

'You and me?'

'There never was a you and me, Peter.'

'You don't understand. I'm not an empty seat any more. I'm different.'

'I have to go.'

MJ got into a taxi. She looked back at Peter. 'You *are* different,' she said, and closed the door.

Betty Brandt took the street cleaner into Jonah Jameson's office. He was carrying something in a brown paper bag. He put the bag on Jameson's desk and took out … Spider-Man's clothes!

'Where did you get those?' shouted Robbie Robertson, Jameson's number two at the *Daily Bugle*.

'In the street,' the man explained.

Jameson couldn't believe his eyes. Spider-Man no more? This was front page news! 'I'll give you $50 for them,' he said.

'Only $50?' said the street cleaner.

'All right, $100. Miss Brandt – take this man away and give him his money!'

It was two years since Uncle Ben died. Peter sat at the table in Aunt May's home and she gave him a cup of tea.

'It was all my fault, Peter,' she said. 'You wanted to go by train that day. Uncle Ben wanted to drive you … and I didn't stop him.'

Peter decided to tell her.

'Aunt May, it was my fault,' said Peter. 'I didn't go to the library that day. I went somewhere else … to win some money … to buy a car. I wanted to look good for MJ. It happened so fast! I won the money, but the guy didn't pay me. Then another man took all the money. I didn't try to stop him. I let him go. He wanted a car … he tried to take Uncle Ben's. Uncle Ben said no and the man shot him. I held Uncle Ben's hand when he died.' Peter was crying now, and he took Aunt May's hand. 'I've tried to tell you so many times,' he said.

But Aunt May took her hand away. She had no words to speak. She looked sadly at Peter, then she stood up and went quietly upstairs.

Down by the Hudson River, Doc Ock was finishing his new fusion reactor. He stood back and looked at his work.

'Just one more little job,' he said. 'All I need now is the tritium.'

Harry Osborn was in his father's old room. He was looking at newspaper stories about Spider-Man. And he was drinking. Suddenly there was a loud noise outside. THUMP! And then another. THUMP! Harry went outside. Suddenly a metal arm appeared. It pushed Harry to the ground.

'Hello, Harry,' said Doc Ock.

'Otto. Wh– What do you want?'

'Tritium. But I need more of it this time.'

Ock took Harry with one of the arms and held him out over the street. The street was a long way down.

'Stop!' cried Harry. 'Bring me Spider-Man … alive! Then I'll give you the tritium!'

'How do I find him?' asked Ock.

'Peter Parker,' said Harry. 'He takes pictures of Spider-Man for the *Bugle*. He can tell you.'

Ock was already on his way.

'Don't hurt Peter!' Harry shouted after him. But Doc Ock wasn't listening.

Chapter 9
Where is Spider-Man?

Peter walked along the street. It was cold and he pulled his coat around him. He saw a newspaper. *'CRIME UP 75%,'* it said, *'WHERE IS SPIDER-MAN NOW?'*

And then he heard people shouting. People were running past him. He followed them and saw a building on fire. Peter was going to take off his street clothes. And then he remembered. He was Spider-Man no more.

'There's a child on the second floor!' someone cried. The fire-fighters weren't there yet.

'Spider-Man no more,' thought Peter. 'But Peter Parker can still help!' He ran quickly into the building.

Inside, he heard the child crying. The heat was terrible. Peter found the little girl and carried her down the stairs. The stairs fell into the fire behind them. Back in the street, he gave the girl back to her parents.

'You did well, son,' said a fire-fighter.

Another fire-fighter came up. 'Someone on the fourth floor didn't get out.'

Peter heard this and he felt so bad.

The next day, Peter got a message from Aunt May. When he arrived at her house, there were boxes of things all over the garden.

'What's going on?' he asked.

'The bank gave me another few weeks,' she explained, 'but I'm moving on … I found a small flat.'

'Why didn't you tell me?'

'I can look after myself, Peter,' said Aunt May. 'And young Henry Jackson from across the street is helping me. He's carrying my boxes and I'm paying him $5.'

'Listen, about my last visit–' Peter started to say.

'We don't need to talk about it,' said Aunt May. 'It was difficult for you to tell me. So, thank you, and I love you, Peter.'

Young Henry Jackson came for another box.

'Hi, Henry,' said Peter.

'You take Spider-Man's pictures, right?' Henry said. 'Where is he?'

'He … er … wanted to try other things.'

'He'll be back, right?' asked Henry.

'I don't know,' answered Peter.

'Henry wants to be Spider-Man when he grows up,' said Aunt May. 'Children like Henry need a hero. We all do! And I believe there's a hero in all of us … making us do the right thing.'

'Does she know?' thought Peter.

Back in the city, Peter took a lift to the top of a tall building. 'Do I still have a hero inside me?' he asked himself. He looked across to the next building.

'I can do it,' he thought. He ran fast to the edge of the roof and jumped. He 'flew' across towards the next building. He felt great. 'Woohoo! I'm back! I'm back!' he shouted. But then he started to fall. Down he went, faster and faster. Luckily there were washing lines between the buildings. He caught one and swung down the rest of the way. He crashed into a wall and fell between two cars. 'Oh, my back! My back!' he cried.

John Jameson and MJ were sitting in MJ's flat. They were getting married soon. And they were talking about their big day.

'Don't you want to invite your friend – the photographer?' asked John.

'He's not my friend. He's just a really stupid guy,' said MJ. She came over to John and looked into his eyes. What was she looking for?

'Put your head back for me,' she said to him.

Then she kissed him.

Once, a long time ago, she kissed Spider-Man this way. This time wasn't as good.

MJ sat in the window of a café with a cup of coffee. Peter walked in.

'Hi,' said Peter.

'Thanks for coming,' MJ smiled.

'Is everything OK?' asked Peter.

MJ found it hard to answer. 'Do you remember … after

my play at the theatre? You *were* different that night. I didn't want to listen. But I've thought about it …' MJ looked into Peter's eyes. But Peter looked away quickly.

'Listen,' he said, 'there's more for me to say. I can't be there for you, MJ.'

'Do you love me or not?' she asked.

'I … don't,' his mouth said. His eyes said something different.

MJ moved closer to Peter. 'Kiss me,' she said quietly. 'I need to know something. Just one kiss.' MJ closed her eyes and moved towards Peter.

Peter wanted to kiss her so much, but he was listening to his spider sense. Something terrible was going to happen.

Suddenly he took MJ in his arms. He pulled her with him to the floor. Half a second later, a car crashed through the big glass window of the café. The car turned over above their heads, then crashed into the floor behind them. They were still alive.

Then they heard a loud noise. THUMP! And then again. THUMP! In the street outside, people were running and crying out. Then Doc Ock appeared in front of them.

'Peter Parker,' he smiled, 'and the girlfriend.'

'What do you want?' asked Peter.

Suddenly, a metal arm moved forward and lifted Peter up.

'I want your friend Spider-Man,' said Ock. 'Tell him to meet me at the Westside Tower at three o'clock.'

'But I don't know where he is,' said Peter.

'Find him, or I'll kill her,' he pointed at MJ. Then he lifted MJ in his metal arms and disappeared through the streets of the city.

Robbie Robertson walked into Jameson's office at the *Daily Bugle*. 'There's still no news about MJ,' he said. 'Sorry, Jonah.'

'It's all my fault,' said Jameson. He was thinking about the Spider-Man stories in the *Daily Bugle*. 'I drove Spider-Man away … Spider-Man was a hero,' he said. He turned to look at Spider-Man's clothes on his office wall. Then he turned back and said, 'Spider-Man was–'

Suddenly, there was a sound like the wind. Jonah turned to look. Spider-Man's clothes were gone! And in their place was a web – a very big web – and a message from Spider-Man!

'Spider-Man was a criminal!' shouted Jameson.

Chapter 10
The El train

Peter put on his Spider-Man clothes. They felt right. He wasn't thinking about *his* problems now. He was only thinking about MJ. And now there was no problem with his webbing. He jumped off the roof of the *Daily Bugle* and swung through Manhattan. Spider-Man was back!

He swung through the tall buildings until he arrived at the Westside Tower. It was three o'clock and Doc Ock was waiting for him.

'Where is she?' called Spider-Man.

'She'll be fine,' said Ock. 'Let's talk …'

A metal arm swung at Spider-Man from the right. Another swung from the left. Spider-Man was falling – fast! He shot some webbing onto the tower. Then he shot some webbing at Ock and pulled – hard! Ock and Spider-Man fell together … right onto the top of an El train!*

* A train high above the street through New York City.

Spider-Man and Doc Ock fought each other on top of the train. Ock broke the train windows and took two people with his metal arms. He threw the people down to the street below. Spider-Man quickly made webs and caught the people. Then Ock moved to the front of the train. SMASH! One of his metal arms broke the front window of the train and the driver cried out. Then the arm broke the train controls. Now the train was going faster and faster. It was going to crash!

Spider-Man had to save the passengers – and Ock knew this. He smiled at Spider-Man and jumped off the train.

Spider-Man used his spider sense to look ahead. The end of the line was very near, and it was high above the water!

He shot webbing onto a building on one side, and a building on the other side. But the webbing just pulled off bits from both buildings. Then Spider-Man shot webbing onto every building. He held all the lines of webbing in his hands. His body was ready to break. The train reached the end of the line … and stopped just in time.

The passengers pulled Spider-Man into the train. They lifted him above their heads. Very carefully, they put him on the floor. Then, slowly, Peter opened his eyes. He saw lots of faces looking down at him. Faces of men, women, and children. And Spider-Man was their hero.

Slowly, Spider-Man stood up. But just then Doc Ock appeared! He pushed Spider-Man to the floor. And this time, Spider-Man couldn't get up.

It was a stormy night and Harry was drinking in his father's old room. Suddenly he turned around and Doc Ock was standing there – with Spider-Man in his arms.

Ock dropped Spider-Man onto a sofa. 'And the tritium?' he asked.

Harry unlocked a secret cupboard. A long metal arm pushed Harry away and took out the tritium. Then Ock disappeared quickly into the storm.

Harry moved slowly towards Spider-Man. He took a knife from his father's desk. His face was white and angry. He lifted the knife above Spider-Man.

'First let's see your face,' he said. 'I can look into your eyes as you die.'

In the light from the storm Harry looked at the true face of Spider-Man. He stood back and dropped the knife.

'Peter! No! It can't be!'

Peter looked into Harry's eyes. He got up quickly.

'Harry,' he said. 'Where is she?' Peter was only interested in one thing. 'He's got MJ!'

'No!' Harry couldn't believe it. 'He only wanted the tritium.'

'Tritium?' shouted Peter. 'He's building the reactor again! When that happens, she'll die. And half of New York will die, too!'

'Peter … you killed my father.'

'There are bigger things happening right now,' said Peter. 'Harry, please! I have to stop him!'

Chapter 11
The fireball

In the building on the river, metal cables held MJ to the wall. 'You've got everything you need,' she shouted at Doc Ock, 'now let me go!'

'I can't let you go – you'll call the police.'

Ock started a fusion reaction. A small ball of fire appeared in the centre of the reactor. It started to grow.

High above MJ, someone climbed quietly into the building. 'Surprise!' called a soft voice. MJ looked up. It was Spider-Man!

Suddenly a metal arm swung towards Spider-Man and he jumped to the floor.

'Stop the reactor, Ock,' said Spider-Man. 'You're going to hurt a lot more people this time.' He tried to jump over Ock to the reactor's cables. But two metal arms threw him through the roof and out of the building. Moments later Spider-Man swung back in. He hit Ock hard with both feet. They both went down through the floor into the water.

The ball of fire was bigger now. It started pulling metal into its centre. It pulled the metal cables around MJ. She screamed as her body flew towards the fireball. Spider-Man shot webbing at her and pulled her back from danger. 'Run,' he shouted to MJ.

A metal arm lifted Spider-Man up and threw him to the floor. Ock then lifted him up by the foot. A knife came out of one of the metal arms – Ock was going to kill Spider-Man! Spider-Man shot webbing around the reactor cables and pulled. As the cables touched one of the metal arms, the energy from the fireball went into Ock. He flew back and crashed onto the floor.

At last Spider-Man pulled the cables out of the wall. He looked at the reactor. It was still going. It didn't need the cables any more. It was getting bigger and bigger.

'Doctor Octavius!' called Spider-Man. Peter tried to think. He showed his real face to Otto.

'Peter Parker,' smiled Otto. 'Brilliant but lazy!'

'We must stop the reactor,' Peter said.

'I can't stop it,' said Otto, sadly. 'I won't stop it!'

'You once told me, "We must use science for the good of the world." These arms have changed you,' said Peter. 'Don't listen to them.'

Peter was right, Otto knew that. Fusion was his dream. But he was ready to leave his dream now. 'Listen to me now!' Otto shouted at the arms. 'Listen to me!' At last he could control the metal arms.

'Now, how do I stop the reactor?' asked Peter. 'Tell me!'

'We can't stop it,' said Otto. 'But … maybe … the river! Drop it in the river!'

Peter turned to the reactor. But a metal arm caught him.

'I'll do it,' Otto said.

Peter turned to MJ. She almost cried when she saw the true face of Spider-Man. It was Peter! Now she understood everything.

Suddenly there was a terrible noise above them. A wall was falling towards MJ. She cried out and Spider-Man was there. He stopped the wall with his back.

'Hi,' said Peter. 'This is really heavy.'

Peter was strong, but he couldn't hold the wall much longer.

'MJ, if we die … ' he started to say.

'You *do* love me!' MJ finished his sentence for him.

'I do.'

Peter gave one great push and threw the wall back. Then he jumped up with MJ in his arms, and they swung out of the building.

Down below on the river, Otto stood alone with the reactor. 'I won't die a bad man,' Otto said to himself. Then he, the arms and the reactor fell deep into the river. It was all over.

Peter and MJ were in a spider web high above the river. 'I think I always knew,' said MJ.

'Then you know we can't be together. People will always want to kill me. If you're with Spider-Man, you're always in danger. I will always be Spider-Man. You and I can never be together.'

MJ looked sadly into Peter's eyes. Then he gave her a line of webbing and he moved her slowly down to a boat below. John Jameson was there. He ran up to MJ and took her in his arms. But MJ was still looking at Spider-Man high above them.

Epilogue
MJ's big day

MJ was wearing a long white dress. It was her big day. John and the Jamesons were waiting in the church. The music started and everyone turned to see MJ.

But it wasn't MJ – it was her friend. She walked up to John and gave him a message. He read it and looked at his guests. What could he do? MJ didn't want to get married! She wasn't coming to the church!

Peter sat on his bed and looked out of the window of his little room. 'Somewhere in the city, right now, MJ is getting married,' he thought.

He sensed something behind him and turned.

MJ was standing in the doorway, in her long white dress.

'Peter … I can't live without you.'

Peter walked towards MJ.

'You think we can't be together,' said MJ. 'But let me decide. It's my life and I want to live it with you. I know it will be dangerous. But … I love you!'

Peter looked into MJ's eyes.

'Isn't it time somebody saved *your* life?' she said.

'Thank you, Mary Jane Watson,' he smiled. Then he took her in his arms and they kissed. Nothing could ever come between them again.

Three police cars drove fast along the street below. He looked at MJ. She smiled at him.

'Go get them!' she said.

SPIDER

Spider-Man 2 came out in 2004. The same team made the Spider-Man film two years earlier. Spider-Man was really popular, but they wanted the second film to be even bigger and better.

Many people agreed that Spider-Man 2 was fantastic! They loved both sides – the action film and the love story. And they loved Peter because he was just an ordinary guy.

Some of the ideas for Spider-Man 2 came from the comic, The Amazing Spider-Man. It was Number 50 and it was called 'Spider-Man No More!' There is a picture in the comic of Peter Parker throwing away his Spider-Man costume – just like in the film.

Film Facts

🕷 Spider-Man 2 was the first action film to make more than $100 million in its first weekend.

🕷 They made 35 Spider-Man costumes to use in the film.

🕷 It took 15 weeks to build Doc Ock's old building on the river.

🕷 They filmed in more than 100 different places. They filmed on street corners in New York. They built new scenes in Los Angeles. They used a train line in Chicago.

MAN 2 ™

The Stunts

How does Spider-Man swing through the streets? Film-maker Sam Raimi used a 'Spidercam'. They put cables between high buildings. The 'Spidercam' camera ran very fast along the cables. It filmed the buildings going by really fast. Then pictures of Spider-Man were put on top. And you really believe he can 'fly'!

> Would you like a job as a stunt actor? What other job on a film would you like?

Tobey Maguire (Peter Parker / Spider-Man) and Kirsten Dunst (MJ) did a lot of their own stunts in the film. Some actors like doing their own stunts because it's fun and it helps them understand their character better. They don't know what danger is really like unless they feel it themselves. Other actors think stunts are too dangerous. That's why they have stunt actors!

> **What do these words mean? You can use a dictionary.**
> action   costume   scene   actor   stunt   character

SPIDER-MAN'S POWERS

How Did Peter Parker Become Spider-Man?

When Peter Parker was in his last year at high school, he went on a school visit to Columbia University. His class looked at 15 very special spiders there. The scientists at the university joined together the genes of three spiders – and made the 15 'super spiders'. While

Peter was taking a photo, one of the spiders fell onto his hand and bit it. Peter Parker changed that day. The strengths of the spider went into his body. He became strong. He got super powers and a special 'spider sense'.

The Spider Bite

Genes from three different spiders were in the spider bite:

The **Salticus spider** is a few centimetres long, but it can jump up to 40 times as far as that.

The **Atrax spider** can make very strong webbing.

The **Misumena spider** can sense danger before it appears.

Salticus spider

Atrax spider

Misumena spider

You can have one of Spider-Man's powers. Which will you choose?

Some of Spider-Man's Powers

Spider webbing is thin but very strong. Spider-Man makes **webbing** as thick as a metal cable, but much stronger. It can even stop a moving train! Spidey can shoot webbing a very long way and swing from it, too.

Spiders have millions of little hairs on their legs. They use these hairs to hold onto walls. Spider-Man can **climb** the walls of New York's tallest buildings!

Spider-Man has **super strength**. He can hold back a train. He can hold a wall on his back.

Spider-Man is famous for his **spider sense**. This is a sixth sense in his head. It tells him when danger is near. When he is in the café with MJ, he knows that something terrible is going to happen. This helps him move ahead of the bad guys.

BUT…

Spider-Man is also an ordinary guy. If he doesn't believe in himself, he loses his powers. Guns and knives can hurt him, even kill him. But Spider-Man is so quick he can move out of the way. And his body can also heal very quickly.

What do these words mean? You can use a dictionary.
power   gene   bit (past of bite)   strength   heal

NEWSPAPERS: HER

The *Daily Bugle* newspaper is an important part of Spider-Man's life. Peter Parker takes photos of Spider-Man for the paper. And almost every day the *Daily Bugle* prints stories about Spider-Man –

Peter Parker in Jonah Jameson's office at the *Daily Bugle*

many of them bad! Newspapers are a very important part of real life today – not only in New York but around the world. But where did they come from? And what is their future?

The first newspaper

The first printed newspaper appeared in 1605 in Strasbourg. Johann Carolus started the paper and he called it *Relation*. At first he wrote every copy with a pen – it took a very long time. In 1605 he bought a printing shop and started to print the newspaper. Now he could make copies very quickly and cheaply. The newspaper business was born!

1605 the first printed newspaper starts in Strasbourg

1621 *Corante* appears – it is the first printed newspaper in England

1631 *Gazette* appears – it is the first printed newspaper in France

1645 the first printed newspaper starts in Sweden (and it still sells today)

1880 photographs appear for the first time, in a New York newspaper

1986 the first national newspaper (*Today* in the UK) appears in colour

1994 the British newspaper, *The Independent*, is the first to also appear on the Internet

...O STAY?

Do you and your family read a newspaper? Which one(s) and why? Will the Internet kill the newspaper?

Newspapers today

Most newspapers in the world today are one of these sizes:

Broadsheet: these newspapers are large and not very easy to read on a bus or a train. They are usually full of serious news stories. Some broadsheet newspapers are: *The Daily Telegraph* (UK), *USA Today* and *Die Zeit* (Germany).

A newspaper seller in China

Did you know ... ?

■ Over one billion people in the world read a newspaper every day.

■ Some newspapers use coloured paper to look different. For example, *The Financial Times* (UK) is pink and *L'Equipe* (a French sports newspaper) is yellow.

■ The name of many newspapers around the world is *Gazette*. This name comes from Venice, Italy, where the price of the first newspapers was one 'gazette'.

Tabloid: these are smaller and easier to read on buses and trains. They usually have stories about famous people, terrible events and lots of pictures. Some tabloid newspapers are: *The Sun* (UK) and *The New York Post* (USA).

Newspapers in the future

Because of 24-hour TV news and the Internet fewer people in the richest countries of the world are reading newspapers. But in other parts of the world, more and more people read a newspaper each day. For example, in China they sell 85 million newspapers every day, and in India, 72 million.

What do these words mean? You can use a dictionary.
print / printed / printing   copy   national   serious   event

Chapters 1-4

Before you read

Use a dictionary for this section.

1 Match the words and meanings.

   brain   fusion   roof   science   seat   theatre   web

   a) This is inside your head.
   b) In a building, this is over your head.
   c) A spider lives here.
   d) You can watch Shakespeare here.
   e) This teaches you how the world works.
   f) This joins two things together.
   g) You can sit on this.

2 Put these verbs in the right sentences.

   control   kiss   shoot   swing

   a) Romeo … Juliet the first time he met her.
   b) The criminal … the shopkeeper and took all the money.
   c) Spider-Man can … from one tall building to another.
   d) This dog is too strong – I can't … it.

3 Look at People and Places on pages 4–5.

   a) What problems does Peter Parker have?
   b) Why was MJ happy to leave home?
   c) What kind of scientist is Dr Otto Octavius?
   d) What kind of scientist is Doc Ock?
   e) Why does Harry Osborn hate Spider-Man?
   f) What happened to Aunt May's husband?
   g) Where can you find the most famous places in New York City?

After you read

4 Are these sentences right or wrong?

   a) Peter loses his job with Joe's Pizzas.
   b) The *Daily Bugle* loves Spider-Man.
   c) Peter hasn't got any money.
   d) Harry tells Peter that MJ really likes him.
   e) Aunt May is not in trouble with the bank.

5 Answer the questions.
- **a)** What does Dr Octavius tell Peter you must do in life?
- **b)** Why does Peter get to the theatre late?
- **c)** Why can't he watch the play?
- **d)** Who meets MJ outside the theatre?
- **e)** What happens when Spider-Man can't shoot any webbing?
- **f)** How does Spider-Man get back down to the street?

6 When Peter leaves a phone message for MJ, the phone cuts off. But he doesn't stop talking. Why not, do you think?

Chapters 5–8

Before you read

7 Which of these problems does Peter have?
- **a)** no money
- **b)** no friends
- **c)** no girlfriend
- **d)** no home
- **e)** no job
- **f)** no time to study

8 Spider-Man can't shoot webbing any more. Why not, do you think?

After you read

9 Put the correct words in the spaces.

angry   build   control   glass   metal   twice   webbing
- **a)** Otto controls his … arms with his brain.
- **b)** The fusion reaction goes out of … .
- **c)** Pieces of flying … kill Rosie.
- **d)** Harry is … because Spider-Man saved his life.
- **e)** Otto and the arms find a place to … the reactor again.
- **f)** When Peter is angry, he is able to shoot … again.
- **g)** Doc Ock drops Aunt May … .

10 Find the mistakes in these sentences.
- **a)** Peter drinks too much at the party.
- **b)** The *Daily Bugle* shows Spider-Man fighting Doc Ock.
- **c)** Jonah pays $50 for Spider-Man's clothes.
- **d)** Harry agrees to bring Spider-Man to Doc Ock.

Chapters 9–Epilogue

Before you read

11 What do you think?
- **a)** Will Peter and MJ get together?
- **b)** Will Doc Ock build a new fusion reactor?

After you read

12 Answer the questions.
- **a)** Who shows Peter that New York needs Spider-Man?
- **b)** Whose kiss was better than John Jameson's?
- **c)** What does Doc Ock throw through the café window?
- **d)** Who dies if Peter doesn't bring Spider-Man to Doc Ock?

13 Put these sentences in order.
- **a)** Doc Ock starts a fusion reaction.
- **b)** Harry discovers that Peter is Spider-Man.
- **c)** MJ decides she can't live without Peter.
- **d)** Peter and Doc Ock fight on top of the El train.
- **e)** Peter asks the real Dr Octavius to stop the reactor.
- **f)** Peter tells MJ they can never be together.
- **g)** Spider-Man stops the train just in time.